A Net Full of Hope

Sue Westwind,
May hope, in whatever form
blesses you, be a constant presence.
Annette
Hope
Billings

ABOUT THE AUTHOR

Annette Hope Billings is an author/actress from Topeka, Kansas where she flourishes despite attempts by the Midwest Bible Belt to constrain her sassy muses. She is proof positive of the diversity and creativity in her hometown. Her family includes her life-partner Dawn, her daughter Tiffany, and two exquisite grandchildren, Kamahra and Kendric. A registered nurse for thirty-eight years, she has always, concurrently, blazed with zeal for writing. Her first collection of poetry, Hope's Wife, was published in 2002 and will soon be re-released. Her work has appeared in Inscape/Washburn University, Kuumba and other publications. She helped to create Speak Easy Poets in Topeka and co-hosts their monthly open mic event. In February of 2014, she was featured in *seveneightfive* magazine in their article "Women Who Rock in Topeka," with a follow-up article in February of 2015. Her passion for theatre has been evidenced by roles in productions of Topeka Civic Theatre and Academy, which resulted in a Renna Hunter Award for best actress. She has also guest-directed three productions of their Studio Series. She has been a long-time member of Table For Eight, a Topeka writing group celebrating its thirtieth year.

Dedicated to my mother,
Mattie Frances Billings,
who taught me
to stand in immense love,
to walk in infinite grace, and,
in lieu of a shadow,
to cast a net full of hope.

A NET FULL OF HOPE
© 2015 Annette Hope Billings

Front cover photograph by Sue Edgerton
Back cover art by Nancy Jones

ISBN 978-1505536621

http://www.anetfullofhope.com
Facebook.com/anetfullofhope

Printed in the United States of America

A Net Full of Hope

Annette Hope Billings

ACKNOWLEDGEMENTS

I am deeply indebted to the countless authors whose words loan voice and meaning to my life when my words escape me.

To Table for Eight, my Topeka, Kansas writing group, I owe you an enormous debt. You have helped me fit these author's shoes.

Warm thanks to Sue Edgerton for the exquisite cover photograph. The magic you do with a camera is parallel to what you do with your written and drawn art. I appreciate you.

Nancy Jones, another fine artist friend, answered my call to create the Ladybug & Lion logo as only she could—with an exquisite eye.

Ra'Yce Martin, when I need a sister-friend to admire, there you were. Your foresight helped give my dream of writing enormous substance.

I am immensely grateful to Karen Overturf and Carol Yoho who gave enormous support to me with editing and cover expertise.

Shannon Kennedy, your faith in me, friendship, technical assistance and lovely prodding provided such lift to this writer's wings. This book would not have happened without you. Thank you so much!

Immeasurable gratitude goes to my beautiful mother, Mattie Frances Billings, for her unfaltering love. Her grace and strength have left such sustaining examples for me. She is gone from this life, but mothering me still. Every exceptional thing about me comes from her. I miss you, Mom.

To my exquisite daughter, Tiffany Walker and my delicious grandchildren, Kamahra and Kendric, bless you. You are my heartbeats.

Dawn Van Egmond, my life-partner, my confidante, and my ultimate encourager—I cherish you for being my loving sunrise. In our love and laughter, I find such hope.

Table of Contents

Writing

Aroused by questions,
art decries drawn conclusions,
adores inquiry.

Where Credit is Due

Maya Angelou was my first preacher, and her writing was the gospel truth I needed as a little girl. The words from the pages of "I Know Why the Caged Bird Sings" were, to me, scripture. My soul was so young and new to this world; I gobbled each word. The book was my manna. And the soul of me, who already knew things no woman, let alone a small, brown-faced girl should know, breathed glory. I didn't know why then, but I sang tight harmony with her story. In deep ways, my life felt like just another verse of hers and a developing wisdom knew those pages would be salve for wounds still in the making. That book was no less than my salvation—and I finished it whole. Had there been no Maya, there might have been no me left for Jesus to save.

Last Word

She ultimately acquiesced
to Death,
the relentless marauder,
but not until she mapped out
her trails to elegance
and to grace.

She wrote the paths as poems,
laid them down on paper tracks
for a lineage of students
taking furious notes.

As she passed through,
she forbade imitation,
insisting readers discover
the marvels they were themselves.

Death pouted to be held at bay,
yet begrudgingly conceded defeat,
ultimately granted Maya
the immortal last word.

Ingress

This crowd of poems,
who loiter en masse on this page,
take many routes to get here.
I labor with them all,
some acutely more than others.

They may present sideways,
squares edging from my circular soul.
A few, contrary and overdue,
linger cocooned in my deep,
reluctant to be born.
Others enter smoothly,
oiled and round,
they ease from me like breath.

The odd ones erupt like a sneeze
unstoppable in force.
A fraction shed like blood,
packed cells, emotions that stain the page.
Scores tap-tap my shoulder,
patient and polite at dawn.
A handful box my ears, 2am,
demand I write them down.

Most feel familiar like they
were my company in womb,
others feel of subway strangers
who just so happen to share my path.
Many leave me giddy,
while the one that follows wrests a toll.
A measure are tsunamis,
currents rife with debris.
One can coat my skin in pleasure,
the very next slathers me with pain.

A fraction ache to the surface,
ears deaf to my protests,
they beg my pardon
while they break my heart.

This crowd of poems
who loiter en mass on this page,
take many routes to get here,
through sheer heaven,
through near hell
through salvation,
through demise.

Once I imagined
I created them,
now I know
poetry created me.

Awake

Awake,
you slumbering genius,
get up,
make art today!

You overslept,
but day still awaits.
Gather your tools, create!

There is still room at the table,
destiny reserves your place!

Nest

Eschewing feathers,
I opt instead
for downy underside of words,
line my nest for poems,
await them there.

Let the Moon Be

What is it with you poets anyway? Can't you just let the moon be? When you wake up to find the moon casting luminosity through your window, just turn over and go back to sleep. It is a mere moon for pity's sake, and even poets need rest. Why worry yourself to make some poem of it? You write yourself into full wakefulness, nullifying any chance for return to REM, knowing full well morning will not delay on your behalf. It will come whether or not you play the writer card. Step away from the keyboard and get back in bed. It is utter foolishness to write when there is sleep to be had and an honest day's work to be done in the morning. Go back to sleep. Tell yourself moonlight is just moonlight. Let the moon be.

Enchantress

She casts poems with abandon
like spells;
flings incantations onto pages
with such earnestness
readers are healed before ink dries.

She writes fearlessly
from hand-dug wells of
deep creativity,
words spewing like an
incandescent geyser
onto parched eyes.

She lays on verses like poultices,
souls cured from the hearing,
solid wood of crosses turns porous
and lay lighter on weary shoulders.

Listeners strain with every cell
to marry DNA to her text
and when they ask what they owe,
she insists, all debt, hers to pay.

Symbiosis

I steady the paper
while words clamor
from my depths,
hoist themselves
onto the page,
a trail of healing
glistening in their wake.

Pen cocked,
I write their escape,
they, in turn,
free me.

Kept

I am as a captive
to your every authored work,
held concubine and hostage
by the way you turn a phrase.

Your titles unravel me,
I become prostrate to prose.
Slain in one poem,
resurrected in the next,
I happily hang on every word.

It is to no avail to release me,
I will remain at your feet,
hardly a prisoner
when I so eagerly stay.

I thrive in grottos of your text,
make my home in crevices
of your manuscript,
sigh, and find delight there.

I am your reader,
do with me what you will,
I wait,
unsated,
for you to write again.

Mishmash

I write this mishmash
of well-intentioned poems,
which sometimes land
askew of targets,
I write them for you who penned me
free of hell.

They are poor homage, such
pale payment
for the vibrant debt I owe.
But, such as they are, they are here—
offerings left with more gratitude
than there are pages to hold.

Thank you, Zora, Maya, Audre,
Alice, e.e., Emily...
I write because you wrote first
and left an estate
of audacious footprints
to guide my timorous feet.

You wielded machetes
disguised as pens
and cleared a path truer than all lies
they used to shackle me.

I surveyed maps you hid in poems,
used keys you slid in prose,
followed the trail of your
word crumbs
to escape this life's dark wilds.

See how I've mined my words from
every place you wrote—

from dirt floors of slave quarters,
gray walls of jail cells,
from margins of unpaid bills,
pink slips,
from subpoenas,
boxes of pregnancy tests,
from ceilings you stared at
as you perished beneath some John?

I write in relative comfort because
you wrote first under duress.
I write unbound from fear,
unhindered by demons
you slew with paper cuts.

I write this mishmash of well-
intentioned poems—for you.

Unbroken

Dreams permeated
with wild horses,
unfinished poems astride them,
corralled by fences
they could effortlessly jump.
Go, I urge them, *go!*
You are not tethered to 8 to 5, like me.

They bolt toward freedom,
stop mid-gallop,
turn, shake heads at me.
No, they say,
we will not go without you.
We will wait here
even if you're kept captive
long, long after five.

We are only as free,
as wild, as you.
Without your words
we cannot run.

Bareback

She rides
bareback astride a poem,
no bit, no bridle,
holds its neck,
face laid against words
braided into its mane,
holds on.

She races
headlong through strophes
gallops full out,
covers more ground
than there are pages to hold.

She slows
rhythm to canter,
breath heated in cool air,
dismounts to walk alongside
lines she has written,
signs name in steam
rising from its back.

Three Short Tales of a Writer

I. Another One Writes the Dust

They, the guardians of 8 to 5, wrung their hands and gnashed their teeth in real worry for her. Once, she was, such a predictable work-a-day captive, wholly obedient to the status quo of how-one-ought-to-make-a-living. But lately, she'd been spotted at coffee shops doing nothing more than day-dreaming and contemplating wall art over some hot beverage of no real importance. When questioned, she answered, "I'm writing," as if that counted as acceptable labor. It was even rumored she'd been dressing in poet shirts and had taken, good grief, to wearing a beret! Oblivious, she was, to the fact beret-wearing people were as suspect as those in hoodies—ne'er-do-wells all. The guardians conspired to stop her. They huddled in secret on lunch breaks and strategized how best to reel her in before the notion of writing was allowed to gel or, God forbid, harden in that soft mind of hers. Their goal, to remind her art is what you do, but hardly who you are. So an APB was issued for her own good, but, once located, she happily pled guilty with that big, silly grin of hers. Too late. She'd already passed over to a land from which real artists never return. The guardians shook their heads and muttered, "Another one writes the dust, another one writes the dust."

II. The Last Transit of Venus

What happened was this—she was not at work that day. They sent law enforcement to get her with sirens *and* the fire department, running hot, stood by—-an aerial truck, no less. Well, it was thought some harm might have come to her because— she did not show up for work. She, who had been working in all punch-the-clock-and-call-me-happy earnestness since age sixteen, simply did not show. She didn't only not show—she did not *call* (work world heresy) and she was the least likely to be a no call/no show as anyone. So everyone was irritated, then worried, then alarmed, then sweaty-palm frantic when she failed to grace her cubicle. Very unlike her, good little worker that she was. Oh, on an off day she fancied herself a (hah!) writer, but no one took that seriously. She was at best a creative drone, a talented worker bee dedicated to honey and hive and she was supposed to be at work that day. So the troops, police and fire, were sent out to rescue, fetch, scold—or whatever the situation required when she was located.

They found her on a park bench, scantily clad, looking straight into the noonday sun, eyes burned. Her face wet with mango juice, which had run down and damped the pages of the Red Chief tablet in her lap. She would have been unrecognizable except for her company-provided lanyard and ID badge. She was conscious, but not lucid and the cops had to pry a number two pencil from her hand for fear she'd harm herself or them. She murmured something about 'a pen and a sword.' They wanted to cuff her, but the firefighters, way more kind, intervened. Her employer was called and agreed to not press charges if she could just make it in by noon and, yes, they would accept her mango-moistened.

"C'mon" the firefighters cooed to her, "your co-workers all miss you."

She was forced to stand, the tablet falling open to the ground. The page read, "The Last Transit of Venus. The End."

III. Blaze

They nicknamed her Blaze. Neighbors pulled her from her smoke-filled home and cooed comfort to her as she mumbled about 'meter and rhyme.' No sooner did she come to than she broke free from their arms and dashed back inside. They hurried after her, calling her name, but lost of sight of her in darkened hallways. Certain she'd perish, and no choice left but to save themselves, they retreated outside. They wrung their hands and shook their heads at her fool-hardy return to such an inferno. Moments later, she stumbled out the doorway gasping, clothes singed. She clenched sheets of paper in blistered hands.

She smiled as she lay in the ambulance—smiled despite the skin that slid away as they wrapped her arms. As they carefully opened each fist, she looked down at the unburned poems.
"They saved me," she said, "they *saved* me, how could I do any less for them?"

They nicknamed her Blaze.

C/O (in care of) the Poets

I hand my dragons to the poets,
they slay them,
lay my tempests at their feet,
they still them.

I cede battles to the poets,
they prevail in them,
drop my mysteries in their lap,
they unravel them.

I release wounds to the poets,
they dress them,
consign my sorrows to the poets,
they console them.

I relinquish chaos to the poets,
they order it,
yield allegations to the poets,
they pardon them.

Liberty from confinement,
sense from my madness,
light from shadows,
bliss from my sadness.

I dispatch my words
in care of the poets,
they write them.

Aperture

I see poems as pictures,
read pictures as poems.
I see images,
moments in time
stalked by a lens,
apprehended by a shutter,
begging for release
so they may pass as time does.

I see captured likenesses
taken prisoner,
denied parole,
confined in 5x7 and 8x10 cells
by digital jailers,
by photo paper—
until my eyes liberate,
each incarcerated moment,
view them as wholly new,
unlived.

I see them
and glimpse history
as if I were there—
there in the living life of it.

Sabbath

Sometimes my Sabbath
is kept at keyboard,
invocations tapped
with devout finger strokes.

I hold high church
on an altar screen
to usher letters
toward hallowed verse.

Sanctified words sing Hallelujah,
consecrated poems shout Amen!

Conduit

My muses, ever faithful
even when I exile them to grow cold
on some remote back burner,
while I shovel too much time,
too much passion
into firing furnaces which I care
little about.

They put up no struggle
while swept to periphery,
to outskirts of my line of vision.

Recipients of my leftover time,
ragged remnants of attention,
odd and ends of my best me.

They accept my weary-
slumped-over-the-keyboard-self,
welcome me like long-awaited
company,
rush to greet me and smile
like I am salve for sore eyes.

They dance me into their presence,
nary a demand for apology,
not counting me tardy,
usher me back to my writeful place.

They take my least,
my tank-almost-empty fumes.
They skim remains of creativity
like cream,
speak words over my ordinary,
hand it back to me remarkable.

Done, they dip deep from
a well of generosity,
insist I pin *my* name to *their* words
knowing, full well,
what a sorry excuse for a poet
I am without them.

I sign my name to art I did not
solely create.
They beam, proud stage mothers
delighted to see their work
attributed to me—
me, who was just blessed
enough to be there
when hands were needed to
write them down.

Betrothed

It is not worries of day
which interrupt my sleep,
it is words at night.

Deep into bedtime,
when sleep should be foregone
conclusion,
I am held awake by poems
who insist I marry them
so they can rightfully carry my name.

I protest,
drowsily itemize my inadequacies,
point out I have too little dowry
to ask for their hand.

But protests serve to encourage them.

"Beloved," say the words,
"we are betrothed to you.
You are the specific poet
of our particular dreams.
You are promised to carry us
over threshold of notion,
set us down on a page,
make honest writings of us all.
This marriage to us, all arranged
so we will not be left unwritten at the altar
to die unspoken old maids.
Now get up and write!"

I protest,
remind them I have only scraps,
only small bones of time,

with meager meat
to pledge to them,
paltry remnants from a day job
which keep me from giving
devotion they deserve.

Those night words shush me,
lead me down aisle to my
writing place.
I vow them every bit
of unclaimed time
and, such as I offer, they accept.

They stand beside me while
our union is sealed
with finger strokes of keys
and as last line is written,
we say, "I do."

Wed to each poem,
I take them bed,
set my alarm,
sleep.

Finished

Having cracked open my bones
and hung marrow out to dry
for all neighbors, passersby to see,
today I'll write some lite-whipped bit
of nonsense,
topped with maraschino cherries
set slightly askew.

No ink for blood today,
no making parchment of my
tender skin.
I will neither delve for meaning
nor rend sense from the senseless.
Intentional superficiality—
the order of the day,
blended with a
deliberate shallowness
to the chagrin of all who think me
incapable of it.

As for dryers?
I forbid them hold a child's
dead body.
I will have them be
for no more than damp clothes.

Then, I will call it good,
say, "Job well done,"
sing myself to sleep.

It is finished.

Sleep, Poet, Sleep

Sleep, poet, sleep,
drop your pen,
rest your head.
Muses will stand guard over
your lot of poems,
repel marauders at the gate.

Sleep, poet, sleep
poems set to sail in your head,
fluttering behind eyes,
nestled in belly,
bear your name
and are safe until dawn.

Sleep, poet, sleep,
poems unstarted,
barely imagined,
poems roughly-conceived
half-finished,
all know your voice.

They will come
in the morning
when you call.

Grief

Widow dark garments
hang threadbare on sad shoulders,
heavy shawls of grief.

Missing

Love we have
for those spirited away by death,
lingers wholly alive
in rich soil of longing.

Sorrow is fecund ground
for celebration of yesterdays,
for storage of recollections,
for nourishment of memories.

So grieve fully
with no constraints,
plant the ache of mourning
in the heart of earth.
Sow "I miss you" deeply,
reap remembrance well.

Red Blinks

Red, in its uppity glory,
exerts itself with no permission
nor warning.

An unapologetic hue,
it enters with flourish.
Upstaged by nothing,
red controls center stage.

Red announces its presence,
demands adoration,
holds its ground.

Opulent, wide-eyed red,
short on humility,
long on sass,
exerts authority,
stares the masses down.

But for grief—for grief,
red blinks
and a careful exam
shows a minuscule dulling
caused by dilution
of wept tears.

For grief,
red will acquiesce,
move downstage
and lovingly
fade
to
black.

(In memory of Paula Elizabeth
Keiser)

In Time

Sorrow unhurried,
calendar says years gone by,
grief says yesterday.

Fresh Grief

This is fresh grief.

Not yet sanded by time,
the point still an arrow,
its blade still fillet-sharp.

This is fresh grief,
its corners are still square,
not enough tears have spilled
to smooth the edges round.

This is fresh grief,
fitting like a thorn-lined cloak,
sticking every breath.
It runs bright red
like uncongealed blood,
flows wild like a river
at odds with its banks.

So let me wail into night,
and keep condolences at bay.
Apply no anesthesia
to my naked bereavement
and remove the timetable
for what no calendar can hold.

This is fresh grief.

On Far Side of Veil

On far side of veil
covering worst imaginable loss,
grieving mother keeps breathing—
painstakingly, reluctantly breathing.

Angels pace perimeter of her heart
securing life-sustaining rhythm
about which she cares naught.

Time,
no match for this sorrow.

Sound of Mother Sorrow

A gasp
turned moan
turned cry
turned wail
turned howl
turned scream
turned sound
turned beyond all ability to be heard

or borne.

Inflammable

Fire in its soulless intent
to lay claim to all available fuel,
utterly destroys what we hold dear.
It leaves unidentifiable remains
of something once known and alive.

With heartless resolve,
it makes what once was no more
with calculating vigor intense as its heat.

It cares nothing about treasured mementos,
nothing of lives too precious to lose,
nothing of skin no match for flames,
nothing of lungs no match for smoke.

It cruelly renders to debris and ash
all we deem treasured and precious,
altering its course to consume
anything left to devour.

Yet after it all,
I still see Lucy *smiling*—
all that was good in her life unburned,
no blistered flesh, no charred bones—
smiling and glad to be free
of a body life-weary
long before flames reached it.

Rendered hot enough,
almost anything will burn—
except for memories
and Lucy's smile.

Tincture

Tincture of kindness,
medicine for my grief,
administered in sips
from spoons of loving friends.

I drink,
rest fitfully,
hoping this remedy
lifts me up
from the depths
where sorrow flung me.

Widows Three

We three widows, widows three,
sometimes in the midst of tea,
pause to wail and dream of thee,
we three widows, widows three.

We three widows, widows three,
gone in search of sanity,
cast our lots in misery,
we three widows, widows three.

We three widows, widows three,
baste in rank uncertainty,
ripe for—what will never be,
we three widows, widows three.

We three widows, widows three,
starched black dresses past our knees
to honor grief's cold deities,
we three widows, widows three.

We three widows, widows three,
move our mouths, but fail to speak,
struggle up the widows' peak,
we three widows, widows three.

Suspend the verse,
worry the rhyme,
break all the rules
in sorrow's time.

We three widows, widows three,
sometimes in the midst of tea,
pause to wail and dream of thee,
we three widows, widows three.

Breaking Through...

Breaking through grief clouds,
gratitude rays streaming through
suns of thankfulness.

Ebullient…

Ebullient Labrador Retriever
scents pungent grief on my clothes,
cocks head in brief question,
decides fetch is still the order of the
day.

Enough

Enough.
Take your flowers, Love, and go.
I am near dust now
and I have no need for them.
No more bouquets to
adorn my marker-
the scents, so heady, so sweet—
are wasted on me.
Keep them for yourself,
bury your lovely face in them
or make a garland to rest
upon those breasts of yours
I like so well.

Enough.
Save your precious tears
for some well-done
romantic comedy.
Take "widow" off your nameplate—
it links to something dead
and you are anything but that.

Enough.
If I had hands,
I would not use them to hold you—
no, I would snip the buttons from
your mourning cape,
lay you bare for all to see how
alive you are.
Go away from here, this
valley of sorrow.
It takes me away from heaven to have
to meet you here.
Don't decorate my grave,
decorate your life.

Enough.
And if you must still gather dahlias,
put them in your hair.
Don't bring them here,
no one need tarry here but the dead.
You have mourned enough.
Take your flowers, Love, and go.
I am near dust now, and I have no
need for them.

Enough.

Words Failed

It was tragedy out of which
I could not write us.
Even while I tried to edit pages
of an inevitable last chapter,
I knew enough of death
to recognize its steps up the walk.

Write as I might,
my verses detained no cancer cells
and the metastatic march proceeded
until my beloved lay beyond my lines.

She died mid-sentence
while I tried to scribble her healing,
leaving poems I hoped would
cure her,
utterly undone.

I buried her, rough drafts in hand,
astounded by how such a war
had been ceded—
when we had come to battle
armed with such brave words.

Permission

I come and sit softly on your bed to watch you sleep. The rise and fall of your chest is like the ebb and flow of waves—waves on the shore of some distant, exquisite sea we did not get to visit. I see your brows knit a frown as you dream of her. You fret you should be dreaming of me. I smooth your forehead and whisper "there-there" sounds you will not remember when you wake. It is okay—entirely okay that you dream of her now instead of me. It is what I want—that every corner of your waking and sleeping life should bear evidence of her. That's my girl— fancy her fully, desire her deeply. Not one ounce of who we were is diluted by your affection for her, nor is one iota of us changed. I remain ever and always as close, as deep, as your breath. I have passed away and you remain wondrously alive. I have no tangible access to you and it is the physical I wish for you. I want her fingertips at the end of yours and her lips pressed on yours. You stir and reach for me and find only thin air, which will not suffice the full woman you are. So don't fall, my sweet, *leap* into love. She is an extraordinary place to land. She will not take my place; she will create her own—making new memories—making you unmistakably as much hers as you were mine. She will pick up where I left off.

When you awaken, draw your heart to full height—and love her—not as much as me, love her *more*.

My hand strokes your face and you murmur a name in your sleep— hers this time, not mine. I smile, intensely relieved. My work here done, I settle the covers around your shoulders. I rise from your bed and go on about my heaven, happy you will awake and go on about your life.

Day Pass

Of course I could not stay, but with a day pass, Could I visit? Just me—no baggage to check; no carry-ons. I would wait at Heaven's gate with all due patience and smile, oh I would *smile* to see you! I would reach for you. So tell me, would my hands pass through or would you wear some familiar flesh just for me? It would be bliss to see you. Would you take me about, introduce me around or would you find us a quiet aisle of paradise? Beautiful as it would be, I'd want no tour—only to see you. We could sit and talk or levitate and I could tell you all my news—poems I am writing, my new grandson. Did he coo at you as he passed by you en route to my arms? Did you slip a note in his soul like a message in a bottle, one he will read me in due time? Is there a place there where I could get a bite to eat and would they fashion manna into sandwiches for tourists the likes of me? You could tell me jokes— from God's lips to my ears and oh, how we could laugh again! And how does time work there? Would I blink and our time would be gone? Would it feel like an instant or the lifetime we didn't get? So many questions! One last one—at day's end, would you walk me to the departure place and remind me you will be there waiting on the day I come back to stay? And send me off with a stole of angel hair? Would you kiss me once on the nape of my neck and remind me not to look back? And of course I could not stay but, with a day pass, surely I could visit?

A Woman of Her Word

A love, long gone,
sings for me
through wind chimes.

I hear her still
after breeze
has died down,
a song after death,
a promise kept.

Lotto

I walk up to the counter and lay a new one-dollar bill, with In God We Trust, face up. God smiles a silent "I-told-you-so" and places the money atop the cash register drawer. "What brings you here, Daughter?"

I stand silent, not surprised at all, in this life of mine, to find God working at Quick Trip. God already knows the answer to the question as clearly as the *lub-dup, lub-dup* of my pounding heart.

"Annette, I hear the answer in your heart, but speak your prayer aloud. Give it life."

I inhale deeply, draw my shoulders back and feel the muscles of my mouth ready to contract.

Praying birth to words— a familiar thing for me, but these gravid ones make me pause. If my life has played out as a lottery, then truly Joyce Lynn Jenkins was my first prize—my winnings for never giving up on love. I understand how infinitely blessed I am, because so many people never win. Many lack the faith to even play. I stand before God, offering my heart and a dollar for another chance at that exact kind of love Joyce and I shared—*again* in the same lifetime.

I speak softly. "Dear God," I say, "I –I – I want to win- the- lottery-again."

God responds, "Say it louder, clearer, Annette."

I repeat it, through tears, less hesitation, "Dear God, I want to win the lottery—again."

God smiles, coaxing me, "Once more with feeling, Sunshine!"

I am weeping now, "Dear God, I want to win the lottery again!"

God opens the cash register drawer and tucks my dollar inside. As my Lotto ticket prints, the bell on the store's door tinkles behind me. I don't turn, but, as someone enters, I feel acceleration in my spirit.

God grins, winks, "Don't look now, Precious, your prize is here."

Anniversary

Annette: It is getting close to anniversary time, Honey. Close to the five-year anniversary that marked the icy slide down into the fifty-nine days between your diagnosis and your death. Is there something I should be doing? Some black I should don for a time?

Joyce: No Love, there is nothing for you to do except stay fully, exceptionally alive—just like I loved you, just like I left you.

Annette: Okay… I still miss you with every breath.

Joyce: Yes, I know.

Square Dance

I saw the Widow Billings doing a jaunty jig in the square last night and, yes; I'm quite certain it was her. The sight of her threw me because— well, there were *peacock feathers* twined in her hair and a red, fringed pashmina spread over her shoulders. She wore a purple poet's shirt, buttoned up just north of indecent, cinched with a leopard print belt. The right hem of her skirt was tucked, just so, into her waistband, so that it draped to show a shameless portion of thick, brown thigh. She was, of all things, *barefoot*, toenails lacquered in "Great Balls of Fire Engine Red" and cowry shells circled her left ankle. Her head was thrown back and she was laughing, no, full-on *giggling* like a 15-year-old, dew-wet girl. And her eyes, those eyes where rivers of hot tears had worn away caverns, were backlit like—like twenty-seven Christmases.

She was not wringing her hands, rather they were loose and free like her feet—fingers outstretched and reaching for something (or someone) outside my line of vision. Yes, I tell you, I'm quite certain it was the Widow Billings, I know her when I see her! As many times as she has paced that very square weeping and talking to herself in grief's thick dialect. As many times as she stumbled about singing a sorrow song that made the bones in my ears vibrate so sadly—her pitch always a little flat, but it is how sorrow should be sung. She would be there all hours of the night while the rest of us slept and made spoons with our wives, husbands, lovers and the occasional casual acquaintance. I would know her anywhere—the forlorn figure she cut, shoulders bowed, head low, heart swollen with all manner of congealed loss. *I know her*, which surprised me all the more to see her dancing so gaily in the square. I stood at my window and watched all night, smiling at the lightness of her spirit. And when dawn came, the Widow Billings waltzed herself right into it—fearlessly—like the *only* question she had was what step to do next. I saw the Widow Billings doing a jaunty jig in the square last night and, yes; I'm quite certain it was her.

Arachnophobia

The woman was perfectly safe
until a Black widow spied her—
until she was spotted by the one
ready to doff her mourning cape.

The woman was in no way at risk
until she breached the radar
of the one who was trading her
wailing wall
for a closer likeness to life.

The woman was clear of harm's way
until she tremored the web
and awoke all eight legs
of the one remembering
how to hunger, to thirst.

Then she became fair game,
just short of prey for the widow
ready to spin again,
enjoy again,
love again.

Mmm hmmm, the woman was
perfectly safe
until a Black widow spied her.

Love and Relationships

Great love requires
only to give all always,
days on end of days.

Right Lane

On this romance Autobahn,
I linger, right lane,
tank fueled with more
caution than rush.

I disdain fellow travelers with my
brake taps,
rear view glances,
check, check and re-checks of maps.

A Sunday excursion for me,
moving on for movement's sake.
Remembering other drives,
other loves whose hands rested
on my thigh with familiarity
and passion.

Go around me if you must,
curse my cruise control,
but understand I must stay
hurry-free
to stay worry-free.

No final destination,
no need for passenger—yet.
I only know to drive,
to live is to drive still—
safely, slowly
in the right lane.

Note To Self

You are either going to do this
love thing
or you're not.

You are going to step out
into the abyss of unknown,
ante up and lay it down,
you are going to give *all*
and want all
and let yourself be bare naked
in full daylight,
with your tender heart exposed
or you're not.
You have never half done love
in your life.

So you know, don't you?
You are either going to do this
love thing
or you're not.

If You Don't Want Deep

If you don't want deep,
I'm not the woman for you.

If you don't enjoy challenge,
then you're not the woman for me.
Now that we've lain that foundation,
can we just do the darn thing?

I will try you-
your endurance
your faith
your understanding—
not on purpose
but just by nature of my me.

I didn't ask to be born a force.
I might have preferred
the easier life of less depth,
but the roots of me
shoot deeply down
into the best of Earth.

So if you don't want deep,
I'm not the woman for you.

In Range of Love

While you are away,
it assuages my soul to know
this yearning for you
is water from a different well.

It holds no bitter burn of sorrow,
no metallic flavor of grief,
no acidic burn of forever,
it tastes only of "I wish you
were here."

It is a drink of sweetness,
sugared by your promised return.
It soothes on its way down,
coats the worry in my throat
with calm.

I still miss you deeply,
but this cup of missing you from
which I drink
does not hurt to hold.

It is wholly bearable to have you out
of arms' reach,
for you remain in range of love.

Barnburner

I assume battle stance,
breath steady,
feet planted,
ready for this twelfth round
of missing you,
determined to go the distance
'til your tall silhouette
graces my door.

Gloves up, head down
I plot my next jab
to the breadbasket.

I glance at my corner man
who nods approval
"*You've got this*," eyes say.

Time and distance
stand opposite me,
throw hooks then jabs
and mistake my jaw for glass.

I, love's determined pugilist,
stick and move,
stick and move,
weary but not feint of heart.

My Love's Laugh

I give thanks for my love's laugh,
an unforecast shower,
a serendipitous spring,
an unexpected brook
bubbling up from her soul
to drench mine.

So Gay

Shared laughter,
anchored in our hearts'
sheltered harbor,
always there
to launch from in somber times.

We board the joyful vessel
at the slightest whim.
Coupled on our deck of mirth
we grin, then giggle more.

Browns

Much is made of blue eyes
and rightly so.
Blue eyes,
of ocean,
of sky,
of Sinatra fame,
warrant high praise indeed.

But when I gaze into the browns
of this love of mine,
it dawns on me
her eyes share chocolate's hue,
the shades of rich soil,
the color of coffee.

In them, I see Autumn leaves
around my feet,
steamed cocoa in mug,
and the coat of a mare
I loved to ride.

In an instant, I succumb
and know I will gladly forego
all ocean,
all sky,
all Sinatra
for the chance to look long into her
browns again.

Matrimony

Unbeknownst to her,
I marry her a little every day
in each loving interaction,
every tender coming together.
I pledge my life to hers
in the great and minutia of our
couplehood,
in the passionate and mundane of us.

I do not tell her we are wedding
because she might balk,
perhaps even withdraw——
not from lack of love,
but from unfamiliarity
with how matrimony works.

I am summa cum laude graduate
of Star-Crossed University
with a double major in love
and romance——
the art, the science of commitment
comes easy for me.

She will eventually ask me to do
what I have already done,
but by the time she realizes it,
she will be already so married to me,
she won't care.

She will lay down all hint of worry
and joyously betroth me back.

Perhaps we will have a ceremony
some fine day,
but we already have a
magnificent marriage,
this bride of mine and I.

She Smiles

She smiles,
stars pout envy
and moon takes note
how best to shine.

She sighs,
lark stops mid-song,
mimics melody
of her breath.

She laughs,
brook amends flow,
tries to impersonate
her gush of joy.

She weeps,
wolf halts half-howl,
scent of her grief
lines its nostrils.

Equal parts
light
air
bliss
sorrow.

She smiles.

Titanium

Steeling itself
against inevitable break,
heart contracts
within lace cage of titanium alloy,
love straining against metal.

Separate Ways

What if we take time
to handle this moment gently,
to hold our peace
instead of clinging fast to pride?

What if we grasp this instant
with kid, not boxing, gloves
and let silence hang
softly in this space
rather than bat the quiet
with non-refundable words?

What if we don't sacrifice calm
for the chance to score victory,
and tread gingerly instead of
roughshod,
letting this union
lay cradled in our hands
rather than trampled underfoot?

What if we trade tenderness
in lieu of slinging barbs,
refuse to shatter this love
into bits too small to mend
and listen fully to questions
not force feed each other answers?

What if we rebuke the ungodly,
elevate the holy?

Maybe then tomorrow
we would still be together
and the path we set out on
would not be called
separate ways.

Pain

Courage contradicts
in opposing direction
as pain beckons *come.*

PAIN

Pain is
an uninvited guest,
a stowaway
skulking in muscles, joints,
lurking in ligaments, tendons
to heckle every effort.
Rude and unseemly,
it does utmost to hinder.

Still I endeavor
and battle
to proceed.

Ouch

Daily the minions of pain
do battle in my body
to see which will be loudest, harshest,
which will intrude most rudely,
which will upstage me the most,
which will leave me most undone
and cause me to clock watch
like an over-zealous sentry.

On a good morning,
while they haggle
and cast lots for control of my day,
I sneak past them,
get on with my joyous life
before they can miss me.

Those days are precious few,
but, live for them, I do.

Key of Hurt

Pain sounds notes
first sharp, then flat
paying no heed
where melody is at.

It gallops measures ahead
or dawdles three beats behind,
to muddle rhythm,
to sully rhyme.

Tries to force duets
where solos should be,
in full voice,
bellows off key.

The gist of the song
is lost because
pain curtseys, then
mistakes protests for applause.

Leading Edge of Storm

Leading edge of storm
barometer hums low song
joints howl pained response.

Dramatis Personae

In these acts of my life,
I make sparse mention of pain.
Still, it steals too much notice
in my grimaces, my groans.

I shan't yield glory of center stage
despite plethora of monologues it
covertly stores.

Pain lays in wait for any
limelight it might commandeer,
petitions for leading roles
I refuse to concede.

So it jeers from offstage
and mimics my lines
while I star in roles
written explicitly for me.

The cost, colossal,
to constrain pain to the wings,
still, the price is no more
than I gladly pay.

Sensuality

Skin to unclothed skin,
a nest of sleeping lovers,
scarcely air between.

Lifetimes

The sound,
the peaceful cadence
of your sleeping breath,
soft front of your spoon
pressed against back of mine.

These, languorous moments
curve into lifetimes.
Eternity, in an instant,
exquisitely condensed.

Fifty Shades of Tea

Immerse me
and let me steep.
Submerge me to submission,
baptize me with dominance.
Make me float—wet, obedient
soaking in, then giving off
heat to you.
Make me wait,
plead to surface.

At your leisure,
pull me out,
ready,
full-bodied,
aromatic
just for you.

Then, dunk me again.

Explicit

She slunk in
dressed in red-on-red lust,
daring me to avert my gaze.
I was clad in restraint.
Our eyes locked and
she mouthed the words, "my prey."

We circled,
leaving moist footprints on wood
floors.
She grinned,
showed a tongue pierced with steel.
We postured in ever smaller rings
her drawing me in,
helpless to resist.

When I was close enough
to share her breath
my last words to her were,
"I give."

PASS (pull, aim, squeeze, sweep)

Concubine of heat,
brightest blue of passion's flame,
love burns hot and clean.

Hues Is It?

Try as I might to make full
rounds of the color wheel,
to dabble in different shades,
to peruse the whole of palettes,
to take heed of entire spectrums,
it is red who woos and controls me.

Brazen red,
not a shade to let me wander far,
uppity red,
who keeps me on a short leash.

Shameless, blatant red,
permits only brief forays,
short encounters with other hues.
Unabashed, bold red,
whispers loudly.

Certain, evident red
leaves no doubt,
needs no explanation.

She resists dilution,
upstages every space,
holds for applause.

Restless red
who won't sit still.
Hungry red,
ever in want of more,
makes me say her name.

Hollow Me Out

Hollow me out,
empty me.
Scoop great handfuls
of what I think I know
about loving you.

Convert me,
a blank page for you,
a clean slate,
to write explicit things—
in ink.

Erase foregone conclusions,
preconceived notions,
make me new for you.

Teach me how to please you,
show me your ropes and
teach this old dog some
carnal tricks.

Hollow me out,
  empty me
    then
      fill
      me
        in.

To Be Known

To be known,
to be taken,
reduced to lowest terms
on your terms.

To be made a fraction
of my former self
by your clear direction
and swift correction.

To be taken out on limb
blindfolded and bound,
nothing but your voice
to orient me.

To trust fully,
to obey wholly,
  to serve,
    to serve,
      to serve
and to be known.

Many Moons

There are moons that chart the
ocean's course,
guiding tides toward waiting shores,
moons that signal planting time
and whisper cycles to women's
wombs.
Moons that worry troubled minds,
causing uprisings
and vexing beasts to howl.

But this night's moon rose
to stir deep longings
in a lover's soul.
Full, ripe, enticing,
a woman's breast of a moon
that seduces the night
and demands we watch.

A moon which pulls passions forth
and agitates desires.
A moon that says to lips, *kiss her*,
to fingers, *touch her*,
to heart, *love her*
for many moons.

Nature

Come like evening,
day ending on silken hush,
awash in color.

Her Name is Summer

Her name is Summer,
rightfully so,
woe to those
unprepared for her heat.

She is a study of extremes,
so oven-esque,
an unrepentant, fiery, furnace
of a girl,
luring the masses
with ideas of scant clothing,
promises of long days.

She stands in season,
unmoved by their discomfort,
while legions melt in her presence
she doles out mercy with a spoon.

The unaccustomed succumb,
the ill-equipped –
doomed to wilt,
still they all gladly pay in sweat
just to utterly have her.

Her name is Summer
rightfully so,
woe to those
unprepared for her heat.

In Season

August steps over
pools of sweat,
lifts hem of her cotton sundress,
rescues it from being sodden
to any degree.

Not yet ready to cede to September,
undeterred by spectacles of distress,
by pleas for relief,
merciless in advance,
she blazes on.

Beckoning Spring

Perched on Winter's edge,
beckoning Spring to arrive,
cold entreating warmth.

Not to Be Mistaken

Not to be mistaken
for older sister Summer,
Spring is purposefully fickle—
runs warm,
then cold
to keep masses off balance.

Half method,
half madness,
she conspires,
so to be all the more
adored when she
finally settles in.

Sprung

I am Spring.
I arrive,
no oath of immediate warmth in tow.

Consistency, absent from my
repertoire,
a hybrid of lion and lamb.
I disrupt plans
for short sleeves, bare legs
with surreptitious blasts of chill
and I relish protests
over retrieval of coats.

Eventually, as it suits me,
I settle into temperate days,
allow my warmth
to siphon chill from bones.

But until then,
I am Spring,
delighted to baffle the earth
and leave the land sprung.

Will You Stay Now Spring?

Will you stay now Spring
or ever elusive be?
Either way, welcome.

Kansas Winds

Kansas winter winds
leave bite marks on tender skin.
But Autumn air blows crisps nibbles,
chilly admonitions
to keep sweaters close at hand.

Winter Leaves

Winter leaves at will,
not to be hurried away,
salutes March with snow.

Concert in Three Notes

Cardinal graces
solitary branch of life,
sings untold longing.

Empowerment

Let no one convince you
to trade an ounce of your joy
for a pound of their promised
happiness.
Happiness ignites quickly,
but joy, *joy* burns long.

Brava!

When they called, "Places!
she refused to debut as "victim."
She made them hold Act I
while she altered her stance.
She called for a Bedazzler
to decorate her scars,
made them print new playbills,
and rename her character "Survivor."

She made her entrance,
found her mark,
upstaged all doubts
she could carry the part.

By the time they called curtain,
roses carpeted her stage.
She bowed to a full audience
who had turned their pity
to a standing ovation.

Switcheroo

I lured the tiger
called fear to my corner,
lifted my head to
expose my neck.

It grinned and leaped
at my exposed veins,
then I turned the tables,
pulled a fast one and
devoured it.

Meadow

When the fields of my innocence
were burned black by abuse,
poems of other poets
covered the taproot of me.
Their words held me safe,
assured there would be enough of me
left to plant again
after the flames of trauma burned by.

When the firestorm ended,
poems brushed away debris
and found me at a loss for words.
They scooped me up and held me,
opened their books and read me well.

They stayed there,
at times my armed guards,
at times gentle guides.
They remained until such time
I could write my defense
should the horror come again.

In time, I was helped to my feet
and poems became rod and staff
until my own two feet had a
familiar feel.
When strangers stopped by
with kind offers of healing rations,
I asked only for more volumes to
fortify my bones.

When news I had survived
reached raiders of tranquility,
they returned to scorch what was left
of the meadow where my soul
still grew.
But I was re-cultivated lush
and strong
and I had my words to stand
in my stead.

My poems answered
when the horror flared again
and called for me at my
meadow's edge.
My words answered in a
powerful voice,
"There is no one you can harm here:
she has moved."

Battle Birds

Oh yes, they came in peace,
those doves who rescued me,
in peace, yet fully-armed.
So armed, in fact, my enemies
slunk away,
bested again by mere birds.

Vacancy

Here in this space is every unworthy, unacceptable, unlovable thing about you. See that it is *empty?* Its former owners left long ago, weary of finding anything with which to fill it. Take the sign down from the door.

Also Ran

She bolted from the gate
with the lot of them,
but the others, well-muscled,
served up their dust.
Their joints, strangers
to wear, to tear,
swiftly left her
in their wake.

She ran on legs
known to too many races,
fell off a pace not
hers to keep.
Making up with honor
what she lacked in speed,
she ran like dead last held joy.

She breached the finish line
long after the others,
only empty stands to see,
stray petals from winner's
wreath across her path.

She stood, chest heaving,
let the wind cool her skin.
Saw how far she'd run,
held her head high
like she'd won it all.

When breath was caught,
pain of running eased,
she took victory lap,
trotted back to starting gate—
ran again.

Epicenter

The epicenter of love
is calling you
by your given name.
Listen.
Trust.
Answer.

What You Allow, Lingers

What you allow, lingers,
what you invite, stays put,
so speak rudely to discord
and its sullen sisters,
turn a cold shoulder to bigotry
in all its disguises,
ignore the bell when jealousy rings,
stop violence at the door
like a stranger,
usher in joy like a long lost friend—
take its coat, its hat,
entertain peace,
chat up passion,
pamper generosity,
give the guest room to justice,
make your life poorly suited for
anything but goodness.
Sweep the porch and place a
welcome mat for love.

When hate knocks, act like you've moved.

Laundry

I hang my soul's garments outside
to dry
in the yard on a line in front of God
and all—
nosey neighbors, total strangers
who drive by slowly to gawk.

Deeply stained articles of my life
flapping in the wind,
irregular edges, scars soaking up rays,
sewn-on patches and unmended tears
obvious to the naked eye.

I put them out there on purpose,
pin them all on the line in defiance,
string them up with premeditation,
let them fly like flags!

This I do in hopes
some splintered spirit
will happen by and see how my
soul's garments
look uncannily like their own –
ones they are ashamed to show.

They will comprehend, such as
they are,
my clothes are clean and worthy of
fresh air and light.

May it release them, embolden them,
dare them to free their own apparel
from dark, dank places
and commit them to warm sun and
crisp winds,
to drape them, in triumph, beside
mine.

Pause

While others were savaged by
flashes of heat,
I flared hot with doubt.
I was assailed by worry,
fidgety about what would
become of me,
no longer secured to moon cycles,
no monthly mooring of menses
to mark passage of time.

Would I float, adrift,
a run-on sentence,
no periods at which to take a breath,
ignored by hormones that
used to govern,
estrogen, elusive after years of amity?
What would I answer to
certain as flow
which came, left with
familiar discomfort,
dogged inconvenience,
that shedding of endometria
marking my time?
What of my aspirations,
would they lie inert like my ovaries,
past tense of fertility?

But in these fruitful years since,
currents of time
have fashioned novel links
to many new moons,
composed fresh cycles
to find rhythm.

I ebb, flow from creative shores
with winds to propel and
liberate me.
 I'm content to bear words
instead of children,
to pass poems
in lieu of blood.

I sail confident,
certain the transition signaled
just an end of chapter
in a book I still write
of a life punctuated with
more characters than one.

My time of month—
every day,
it was merely a pause,
not a hard stop at all.

Belongings

I was told to pack quickly: a deluge was coming. Waters were rising.
There was only time to save the dearest of things. I was admonished to
take only what I must; the rest would be swept into deep caverns of
memory. I hurried through my life grabbing what was within easy
reach and what I had to stand tiptoe to retrieve. Here was my chance
to salvage only the best of my life and allow all unpleasantness to be
carried far from me.

As the swells breached my doorway, I held the sack full of my life
above head and waded through to higher ground. Safe, I opened the
bag I had held so tightly that my fingers cramped and palms were
bloody where my nails had dug in. I sat cross-legged on a crest of a hill
and emptied the contents in my lap—eager to see precisely what I had
deemed worthy to save. Which parts of my life, with only the shortest
of notice, were precious to me?

There were the expected things—iridescent joys and shiny
accomplishments, gold-flecked times of contentment and flawless
prisms of peace. But, from deep in the bag, things came that stuttered
the breath in my chest—midnight blue sorrows and serrated grief,
coarse grains of sadness and a locket of despair. I had unknowingly
grabbed sweet *and* bitter. Salvaged both raucous laughter and explosive
sobs. I had chosen shades from the full of life's spectrum, both brights
and darks.

I examined my collection—pieces and bits of my entire life. I turned
each item over to appreciate every angle. I decided to carry it all
forward, to value each thing, to begin anew and call them all my
belongings.

Justice

A clear song echoes
in souls of those will hear
refrains of justice.

All Aboard!

There is a train
bound for justice
with nine seats reserved,
building up steam
solid on the tracks.
Won't leave the station
unless the majority is on it.
Tell me, justices,
will you ride?

Upon DOMA's Demise

Contrary to popular belief,
despite the spoon-fed rubbish
meant to distress the masses,
none of the rumored
catastrophes occurred.
Armageddon was a no-show,
the plagues did not come.

Marriage remains marriage—
only better,
family remains family—
only stronger
and justice remains justice—
only broader.

Nothing is in the loss column,
but wins number beyond count.
Soon the other side will understand
they can relax, exhale
and take a deep, deep breath
of what is right.

Who Knew?

Every mother's son
lay dying in the street,
brightly-colored candy orbs
punctuating his blood.

Who knew the cost of Skittles
had become so high?

Who knew?

(in memory of Trayvon Martin)

Bogus

I know justice,
this is not her,
nor is it even
her evil twin.

I've seen justice
roll down like waters
and the waters were not fouled
like these.

I've met justice,
clasped her hand,
looked in her blind eyes
while she smiled.

This is not justice,
she is no kin,
no matter that she claims to be,
despite the masses bewitched.

I know justice,
this is not her.

Sleepless

I lay awake in hopes of respite
from day's travails,
counted my way through sheep,
through blessings.
I began to count abducted Nigerian
schoolgirls.
and rose to write of them,
but words stuck sideways,
wedged between horror and rage
like a bone transverse in my throat.

I never slept.

Oh Madiba

Oh Madiba, my tata, your funeral is
today and my poem for you still
stutters in my chest.

*Daughter of mine, not to worry. Every word
you have written has traveled on the back of
dreamers who swam seas to bring them to
me while I still had eyes to read them. To
honor me, write your poems for the living.*

Yes, yes, Father, I will.

(For Nelson Mandela)

Cobbler

A poor excuse for a poet,
still nary a Michael Brown poem
put to paper.
Half out of my mind with words
which ricochet between news
he was bound for
grandmother's house
and how he lay in the street
hours after death,
body baking like peach cobbler
in August oven.

Medley

.

Ears gorge on music,
ravenous for harmony,
gobble melody.

Interlude

There, just right there,
captured in the electric cleft
between fingertips and piano keys,
suspended in the expectant space
between bow and cello strings,
nestled in the warm air between mouth and
French horn,
fixed in the potent pause between
drumstick and drum—
there, just right there,
music waits.

In those languid moments as the musician
sojourns spellbound on bench,
engulfed in creative reverie,
there, just right there,
art and artist convene.

As she gracefully hovers
just shy of keys
poised to emancipate sound
by the laying on of hands,
there in that interlude,
the spirit's song resides,
the heart's aria makes its home.

Music emerges long before
one note is confined to paper,
before one chord is struck
or coaxed forth by percussion,
or breath or bow.
Music commences in the promise
made by instrumentalist to instrument.

Like a laboring woman looks
to her midwife,
the song beseeches, "Deliver me!"
And with passionate kiss of fingers on keys
the music is eased into our expectant ears
arriving newborn each time it is played.

Music begins ages before we hear it,
its nascence in the heart of the musician.
In the deep of their breath
it stirs and follows a course of glory
to exit through brilliant voices,
through blessed hands.

Each instrument just a holding place
a stopover, a conduit
for music which is ever all around and
within us
awaiting the peace,
the shalom,
the Namaste,
the runyararo
where it presents its soul to ours—
simultaneously ancient and new,
a mysterious gift from a Divine giver,
the voice of Sacred,
music to our ears.

*Runyararo is Shona for "peace."

Living Thanks

I am the Earth's,
conceived in the exact estate as stars.

I am offspring of her creativity,
end result of her generosity,
consequence of her diversity on
display.

She rocks me in the graciousness of
the wind's caress,
waters me in Spring's warm rain.
Her trees shelter me,
her fields, my solace, my sanctuary.
Her sun blankets me.
She sighs and, in night's nest of
darkness,
I find deep rest.

The earth moans oceans and her
waters buoy me,
she throws back her head
and laughs my spirit into a waltz.
Her tides teach my breath to rise,
to fall in sustaining rhythm.
My heart follows her lead—beats
true—
nudging life through tributaries of my
body.

I consider my arms her branches,
my fingers, her leaves,
my feet, her roots,
my spirit, her fruit.

It is more than duty to honor her,
it is my utter delight,
my pleasure to safeguard her,
my glee to celebrate,
to repay her kindness by protecting
her,
cradling her as preciously and
precisely as she cradles me.

Let me be found not just giving
thanks to her,
but *living* thanks to her,
esteeming her as valuable as my
breath
as sanctified as my blood,
fouling nothing of hers,
esteeming everything.

More than lip service,
I owe her *life* service
so I will grow as sacred as she.

I am the Earth's,
conceived in the exact estate as stars.

Next of Kin

A list of names,
a recitation of lives,
lost, but still remembered.
Sons and brothers,
daughters and mothers
who left us then in droves
and now still slip away
less noticed, but no less missed.

What have we left to embrace
other than our sorrow
which strains our hearts to hold?
We have that stubborn song
sounding in every spoken name,
a persistent pulse louder than loss,
a relentless reverberation
stronger than grief,
an enduring echo deeper than death.
We have hope.

Hope, the generous estate
each person left,
a richness we inherited
so, we, as heirs of their courage,
can doff our mourning capes
and live.

So we, next of kin, may reorder
our grief into bravery
to fight the adding of more names.

So let us speak their names
into the night,
and remember their lives into the day.
Let us speak their names
through tears
and honor their lives through hope.

(for World AIDS Day)

Ordination of Joy

In a season of Autumn grandeur,
God's glory resides in every
vibrant hue.
Amidst the change, we see
God's steadfastness
in every leaf dropped,
a reminder that in the letting go,
we experience our
strongest hold—on faith,
we begin to understand
the changing landscape
signals God's intent to bless us when
we most need it,
we are reminded in this
transformation time,
grace occurs precisely in the
nick of time
and in due season,
our every thirst will certainly
be quenched,
every need met,
every covenant kept.

We are all called
to minister,
to love,
to live the blessed "Yes, send me!"
of service to each other.

As we answer the call,
our paths shall be carpeted with joy
and peace shall light our way.
Mountains and hills will sing choruses
while trees keep time with
clapping of their limbs.
We will become the evidence,
the proof of God's word in us
as we yield, not weeds of
condemnation,
but flowers of grace
and forests of mercy.

Common Knowledge

Children share a delicious truth
with us,
for which there are no words,
hidden in the wattage of the smiles
we exchange—
a nameless, common knowledge,
theirs, anchored in innocence
of not yet having seen it all,
ours, anchored in experience of
seeing it all
and still believing life is divine.

Matriarchs

With generous amounts of elegance,
liberal helpings of grace,
come a bevy of wondrous women
into winters of their days,
leaving footprints of faith,
trails of wisdom in their wake,
showing how great age looks,
telling how living well is done,
modeling resilience,
teaching courage,
shining in such ways
stars should be named for them,
planets rehung in their honor.

Note how they reign.
Time, having given up on dimming
their beauty,
blesses them, instead, with eternal
loveliness!

Wondrous women,
proof that aging well is distinction
and growing older, sheer wealth.

Unfailing

I do not take lightly what they say about my mother's ailing heart and its worrisome congestion. Nurse/daughter that I am, I could recite the implications of leaky heart valves by rote. Still, it riles me to watch them try to write her off like milk past its expiration date. I know her heart full well: I came into being due south of it in her womb. It played the premier rhythm to which I slept and grew. Fetal me listened raptly with developing ears and modeled my pulse after hers.

I listen to their well-intentioned admonitions, "She *is* 90, you know."

I concede I hold no medical degree, but still consider myself an expert witness to testify on her heart's behalf. While they discuss her "poor ejection fraction" and "weakened myocardium" in low tones, I suppress a knowing smile. As love is my witness, I know her heart will stop someday, *but it will not ever fail.*

In memory of my mother, Mattie Frances Billings, April 14, 1922- June 30, 2014)

Call When You Get Home

"Call when you get home," is what she said as always, while I walked to my car a few nights ago.

"I will, Mom," was my rote reply. She stood at the door and watched until I was not only in my car, but backing out of her driveway. I paused at the street, not wanting to leave until I saw that she'd closed and locked her door. We were fixed there for a moment, me watching her watch me—a stalemate as both of us was determined to secure the other's safety before another move was made—each fiercely protective and keenly aware of the other's vulnerabilities. A smile ached out of me in that moment as I saw her lingering at the door and I breathed in how immeasurable my mother's love is for me. I let my eyes drink in the full sight of her standing guard, keeping watch *still* at almost 92— frail but steadfast. Nothing in the precariousness of her health could negate the fact that she would still move heaven and earth to protect me—still fight a bear for me. Only when I blinked my lights twice (our signal for "all is well") did she go in and close her door.

I thought about superheroes on my drive home and how the likes of Super Man or The Rock come to mind for many. But, my super heroine stands at the door, at almost 92, leaning on the doorposts for support, watching me walk to my car, daring anything or anyone on earth to harm me.

Reality insists I steel myself for when my mother's doorway will stand empty. I resist because I have no frame of reference for life as a motherless child. Perhaps I will take long drives after she dies. I will drive well into the evening weeping and giving thanks for the years I had her. And when darkness inevitably falls, I will blink my lights twice—and go on.

An Index of Titles/First Lines

Made in the USA
Columbia, SC
02 August 2017